I0463354

BRAINWELL!

Your Guide to Happiness at Work

Nancy Attrill

www.AdvantageWorkplaceIntegration .com

Copyright Notice

Copyright © 2017 by Nancy Attrill. All Rights Reserved.

No part of this publication may be replicated, redistributed, or given away in any form without the prior written consent of the author/publisher or the terms relayed to you herein.

Nancy Attrill, Advantage Workplace Integration
London, Ontario, Canada
www.AdvantageWorkplaceIntegration.com

The recommendations in this book are for general information. The author does not diagnose, heal, treat or cure any medical or mental health condition or disease.

Each individual is responsible for his or her own wellness path.

First Printing, 2017

ISBN-13: 978-1542859585

ISBN-10: 1542859581

Printed in the United States of America

Contents

Introduction

The brain is a beautiful thing. We so often take it for granted and don't pay much attention to it, until it is not operating properly. Many executives are beginning to believe wellness training is a driving factor in employee retention and improved client service. Since everything we think and do starts with the brain, we should take every action possible to keep it healthy!

Richard Branson says, "Take care of your employees first and they will take care of your clients", placing priority of employees' wellbeing and happiness over client satisfaction. If executives believe this is true, companies should be investing substantial resources to that end.

Employee attrition is an issue in this world of instant gratification. Investing in employees' happiness along with solid client service standards is the key to success. Many in the workplace stay with one company under 5 years; much less if their needs are not met.

This book's purpose is to provide several strategies for employers and employees alike to maintain healthy brain function in a stressful world, be happier and more productive, and ultimately be more successful!

Sleep

Sleep is number one on the list of health strategies, especially for the brain. **Sleep affects our mood, focus, memory and physical well-being.** When we do not get quality sleep, most everything else suffers; when we do, life is better. It's that simple... but wait, it is not, especially when you have tried "everything" and just cannot get that quality sleep you know you need. First, let's look at how the **lack** of sleep affects our daily lives:

Cranky, irritable.

Can't focus or concentrate on tasks.

Distracted driving (and use of machinery.)

Constantly hungry, weight gain.

Relationships suffer (work and personal.)

Immune system is compromised – frequent colds/flu.

Ongoing sleep problems can result in depression, cancer, heart disease and digestive issues.

Do any of these problems remind you of when a child is sleep-deprived? The effect of lack of sleep doesn't change when we become adults. We have learned to control some of these behaviours, but it does come to the surface at times. I am sure you have heard, or perhaps said, "Sorry I reacted badly... didn't get much sleep last night." When our children are sleep deprived, we put them to bed... how about giving yourself the same care?

When we get **good quality** sleep this is what to expect:

Elevated mood.

More productive... clear thinking.

Happier, relationships improve.

Physical energy and mental health improve.

Life is better!

When we are ready to go to sleep, often our bodies and eyes are tired, but our brains are working overtime! We cannot shut it off like a light switch. Think of it as a dimmer switch that gradually gets quieter and quieter as the evening goes on. Therefore, all vigorous activities, both physical and mental should start to wind down after dinner. **Here are a few tips:**

Plan your more vigorous activities earlier in the evening and less vigorous as the evening progresses, creating the "dimmer switch" effect. This way the brain gradually calms the high frequency brainwaves and increases the lower ones which are optimal for sleep.

Plan your next day the night before. Fill in your day planner either before you leave work or at the latest right after dinner. When your next day is planned, you will be less likely to worry about it at 2 a.m.

Turn off all electronic devices at least one hour before bed. These devices are very stimulating to the brain and can contribute to poor quality sleep if used right before bed. Instead, read something interesting and not too aggravating (no work-related reading before bed please!)

Make your bedroom dark for sleep. Your brain's sleep rhythm is on a 24-hour clock (circadian) and it needs dark for sleep (to produce melatonin[1]) and light for waking hours. The brain's Pineal Gland, which produces melatonin, is light sensitive and therefore needs darkness to do its job. In the morning, throw open the drapes or blinds upon rising and it tells your brain to stop producing melatonin. When we experience natural daylight during the day, our brains produce serotonin, which keeps us alert and in good spirits. This is why taking a walk in nature is so important for our health.

Turn your bedroom into a sanctuary. Put your favourite items that are pleasant and calming in the room. Invest in comfortable bedding, a good mattress and pillows that support your head and neck. Do not engage in any negative talk or activity in that room. Entry should be by invitation only (that means kids and pets.) Yes, pets. I am usually glared at when I suggest this to audiences. If your

---

[1] Melatonin is a natural supplement but did you know it is a hormone? The danger of taking melatonin on a regular basis is that you don't know how much you need, may take too much, and disturb the balance of your other hormones. Also, the brain will stop producing its own if it is taken regularly and that may cause a dependency!!!

pets sleep with you and they disrupt your deep sleep patterns, nothing you try will help your sleep until you remove pets from the bed. Kids don't need to access you while you are in your room unless it's an emergency. They are trainable!

Your brain will adapt to this environment and eventually start to automatically calm itself when you enter that room, because the brain loves habit and consistency. So be sure to stay consistent with the calming theme. You can retreat to your sanctuary any time you need to be quiet and alone, either to read, meditate, listen to soft music, love your partner, or just sit on the bed and stare at the wall and chill! It's your special place of peace!

Stop eating for the day at least 2 hours before bed so all food has passed through the stomach before you retire for the evening. This will avoid bloating and acid reflux when you are trying to sleep.

Workplace Habits

Think about all the pressures we are under from the time we awake until we (try to) go to sleep at night; some put upon us and some self-generated. Life is extremely fast-paced for most of us. Do you wonder whether you will ever get a break?

Chronic stress has been proven to be at the core of most illnesses and diseases, physical, emotional and mental. Our cortisol (stress hormone) spikes when we have stress, intended to put us in a fight or flight mode, which is good, but only in the short periods when we need it.

When we experience ongoing stress, this hormone stays elevated, creating a huge burden on our emotions, promoting inflammation, and eventually breaking down our physical health by taxing our immune system. It can be responsible for high blood pressure, diabetes, heart disease, cancer, depression, insomnia, and auto-immune disease, to name a few. How do we address this?

Take time out to chill... give ourselves a quiet break (yes, we all have time for this!) When we go to a quiet place and close our eyes, visualizing a peaceful and calm place, it gives our brains a much-needed break from the estimated 70,000 daily thoughts it processes. 10 minutes x 2 per day will do wonders to help reduce stress, especially during the work day.

Don't eat junk! Make sure your diet is healthy, including healthy fats, protein and lots of variety of veggies! Cut out the sugar (it spikes cortisol!)

Don't "drink" away your stress. Yes, it feels good to have a few drinks with co-workers occasionally to blow off some steam, but please don't be fooled. Alcohol is a depressant and although you may feel good at the time, you may feel down the next day, which defeats the purpose. Moderate your social drinking... it can turn into a problem if you rely on it solely for relief of stress!

Use your allotted vacation! We all need time away from the day to day routine to rest and recharge. Also, take your daily breaks at work. Move away from work for 10-15 minutes in the morning and afternoon, and eat your lunch away from your desk or work area.

Get and Keep Organized – when there is chaos on the outside, there is chaos on the inside and vice versa! Being in control of your workspace is critically important to complete work tasks with ease.

Letting Go (aka Take Out the Trash)

Negative thoughts and feelings not only are harmful to our mental and emotional health, but they can also have a profound effect on our physical wellness. Have you ever noticed chronic complainers are frequently ill, always something "wrong" with them? Their brains are reacting to negative forces which permeate into every area of their lives. This is not to say those with a positive attitude never become ill, because there are other factors to physical health. Why decrease your chance to be healthy and happy simply by your thoughts and words?

Release negative thoughts and memories and send them down the river! All those recurring negative memories can rob you of energy you need to power your brain for important tasks such as focus, attention, mind/body connection and relationships. Negative thoughts are like poison. When we have a thought, a certain part of our brain is engaged. When we speak that thought, however, several parts of the brain are affected, rippling throughout our entire being.

Donald Hebb, a neuropsychologist, believed that neurons which fire together, wire together. What he meant by that is that groups of neurons connect in our brain because of life experiences.

For instance, whenever we think a thought or have a feeling or physical sensation, thousands of neurons are triggered and they all get together to form a neural network. The brain learns to trigger the same neurons with repetitive thinking.

Remember what Grandma used to say, "If you have nothing good to say, say nothing at all!" This is easier said than done. Personally, I am a work in progress in this category, but while I continue in my effort for self-improvement, I find my overall wellbeing is enhanced.

When we hold onto negative thoughts and experiences from the past, we crowd our brains with data which in turn expends energy. If we dwell on it, we are wasting our brain power on past activities over which we have no control. I suspect most of us wish we could just get rid of this pain. Take out the trash! It is much healthier to acknowledge the thought, process it and then let it go. It is not necessary to act upon every thought we have. Consider the consequences at work if we did!

As previously mentioned, we have on average 70,000 thoughts per day... how many of yours are positive? Here are a few suggestions for releasing unwanted memories and feelings:

Relax and let go! Ok, but how? Take three slow, deep breaths, exhaling very slowly, with eyes closed. When we release our breath very slowly, tension in the neck and shoulders is relaxed, especially after three times! Then think about inhaling light and peace, and exhaling negative. Acknowledge the thought, memory or feeling you wish to release. Acknowledge but do not dwell on it. Once you accept the thought, let it go... watch it go up in a helium balloon, or washed out to sea. Continue to breathe in the positive and release the negative. Think about a calm, peaceful place and dwell on it for about 10 minutes. An alternative is to simply say the words "positive" (inhale) and "negative" (exhale). It may take practice but it works. This is a similar technique to the start of meditation, which of course is an excellent way to release stress.

Unresolved issues can take over your mind and cause much anxiety. Whenever possible, confront the issue and find a resolution to it. It may be as simple as having a short conversation with someone, or it may take time to work through the problem. More about that later.

Crowd your mind with gratitude. First thing in the morning, list all the positive things in your life for which you are thankful. You don't have to write it down, but when you do, it helps your brain remember them. It's more pleasant thinking about these things than all the negative... agree?

Feeding Your Brain for Performance

We can maintain good brain health by what we eliminate and what we feed it daily. We have heard many reports that chemicals and processed foods can damage our brain, including eating too much sugar, additives and artificial sweeteners. There are numerous studies that suggest we eliminate, or at least significantly reduce our sugar intake. Here are links to a few of them:

High Sugar Diet Can Be as Damaging to the Brain as Extreme Stress!

(http://www.dailymail.co.uk/health/article-3450298/High-sugar-diet-damaging-brain-extreme-stress-ABUSE.html)

Can Sugar Make You Stupid?

(http://news.nationalgeographic.com/news/2012/05/120522-sugar-stupid-rats-high-fructose-corn-syrup-health-science/)

Reduce Sugar, Reduce Cancer Risk

(http://www.foxnews.com/health/2016/01/06/stu

dy-links-sugar-to-cancer-how-to-reduce-your-risk.html)

If you took the time to read these articles, you will easily see **sugar could very well be the #1 health hazard that is easy to avoid**. We breathe toxic air, we drink water which may contain chlorine and fluoride, and in some cases, we individually cannot avoid these potential health risks. **We can, however, shift our eating habits to reduce our sugar intake.** Some studies suggest we limit the amount to 25grams. Others suggest less.

Hidden sugar is in most processed food products so it is important to carefully read labels. As a new grandma, I have read labels on baby food and discovered to my dismay that some brands of baby cereal contain added sugar! Thankfully there are products available for babies that do not, so do your homework when you go shopping for all food. Processed and packaged food almost always contains sugar in some form. Here are some "hidden" names for sugar – fructose, agave (yes, it is pure sugar and not a health food!), corn sweetener, corn syrup, dextrose, fructose, fruit juice concentrates, glucose, high-fructose corn syrup, invert sugar, lactose, maltose, malt syrup, raw sugar, sucrose, sugar syrup, cane crystals, cane sugar, crystalline fructose, evaporated cane juice, corn syrup solids, and malt syrup.

It is always better to **make your own food** so you can control the sugar (and salt) content. For example, I buy plain full-fat yoghurt and add my own fruit, or sometimes maple syrup, to my taste. I know exactly how much sugar I am getting. Please note, low fat or fat free products usually contain sugar and/or salt to replace the fat! Low fat products also become processed food, which likely have additives which may be unhealthy... again, read your labels!

If you have heard diet experts suggest you only **buy foods from the perimeters of the grocery store**, in other words, avoid canned and packaged food, that is very good advice. You still must read labels of "natural" products as well. Getting back to yoghurt, I am hard-pressed to find decent yoghurt that is not low-fat, nor containing added sugar. 90% of the yoghurt on the shelf is processed and full of sugar! You can always find a good plain and natural variety, but you must look for it!

I think you got the message about sugar! We should also **focus on what TO eat, not just what to avoid**.

What can you do to feed your brain?

Turmeric – There are too many studies to even mention here that prove this natural spice has many benefits to the body and brain. Over 800 studies worldwide are suggesting this should be part of everyone's diet (or supplementation.) It is particularly great brain food due to its incredible ability to reduce inflammation (yes, good for the joints and heart as well.) It is also an effective liver detoxifier. I strongly suggest you take the time to investigate the benefits of turmeric (curcumin.)

The brain is made of water, protein and fat. Along with plenty of veggies (green leafy too,) be sure you **drink plenty of water, eat enough**

protein (but don't overdo it) and include healthy fats (i.e. coconut oil, olive oil, avocado, fish oil-omega 3 with high DHA.) Again, avoid anything processed.

The **lack of Vitamin D** has been connected with depression and Seasonal Affective Disorder (SAD) among many other issues. This is another reason to go outside and be exposed to the sun for 15 or 20 minutes (use caution with children or if you burn easily). The natural Vitamin D from the sun is always the best but if that is not possible, supplementation is an option. Again, use extreme caution that you do not overdose. Consult your family health practitioner for an amount right for you.

Healthy Gut = Healthy Brain – many studies have suggested this strong connection between the gut and brain. It is difficult to maintain healthy brain function if your gut is full of harmful toxins and bacteria. One way to reduce these risks is to eat good quality pro-biotics and pre-biotics every day. Probiotics (i.e. yoghurt, kefir, kombucha beverages, fermented vegetables) multiply the good bacteria while killing the bad, and pre-biotics (i.e. yams, onions, garlic, leeks) feed the good bacteria to prevent parasites and maintain healthy flora. They also convert into B Vitamins which are critical to good health. You can also use supplements if you cannot get enough through your diet, and again, be sure you are purchasing good quality (cheap is NOT always the best). Holistic practitioners are very good at discerning the quality of various strains and brands of pro/pre-biotics and I will not attempt to rate them here.

The suggestions above and throughout this book are for general information only. Always consult your health care provider before making any dietary changes or adding supplements to your diet.

Exercise, It's a "No-Brainer"

Exercise is good for the brain because everything good for the body is also good for the brain! When we stimulate the brain, we are helping it perform better.

Exercise your brain by doing the following each day:

Learn something new, whether it is an online course, musical instrument lessons, or taking up a new language. It stimulates the neuro-networks and slows down the aging process!!

Walk at least 30 minutes per day, preferably in a nature setting. Mall walking in the cold weather will also have benefit, but being outdoors and breathing fresh air will work wonders for clearing the mind! Biking and roller blading are also great options!

Do **stretching exercises** first thing in the morning to increase circulation and blood flow/oxygen to the brain.

Dancing is great exercise and adds fun, which in turn elevates mood. Shake that bootie!!

Mom (or dad, or grandparent) and tot exercises create special bonds that last a lifetime, also elevating mood!

Practice positive thinking. Take time out of your busy day to be grateful. This exercises the brain in areas of mind/body connection, so important to our wellbeing!

Get Up, Stand up! If you work at a desk and sit all day, you are at risk of developing health issues. Studies are proving that prolonged sitting can take years off your life, and increase your risk of heart disease, not to mention reduction of physical fitness. Even if you work out for an hour in the morning and think you can sit or lay on the couch the rest of the day, it doesn't work that way. Sitting the remainder of the day negates any benefit the workout has done. It's that serious. It's important to get up at least once per hour and move around. This will increase oxygen to the brain which will help you maintain the brain power you need to be more productive during your day. I like to stretch and move my arms and legs to change their position and blood flow.

Stress and Anxiety

Ongoing stress or a traumatic event can create a feeling of anxiety, when your mind will not slow down, and you are filled with worry and fear. High anxiety can cause interrupted sleep and possibly lead to depression. **In North America, some studies report at least 1 in 5 adults suffers from either anxiety or depression, or both, and the lost health care costs and lost revenue due to stress-related absenteeism is staggering!** I will not quote numbers here because they vary per different methods of collecting data. Suffice to say, it's a big problem in our society. Children also can develop anxiety due to school and peer pressures.

Are you still awake at 2 a.m. thinking about work? "I have so much to do... I hope I don't forget to ___fill in the blank," etc., etc.

Try planning your day the day or night before! At the end of each work day, fire up the day timer (electronic or paper) and prioritize everything you wish to accomplish the next day, both business and personal. Assign appropriate time, and include 15 minutes between major tasks. This is not intended for you to use for personal business, but rather it gives you a cushion of time to allow for unplanned interruptions and keep you on track. You should always, however, schedule your regular allowable breaks including lunch. Get it all scheduled and let it go. No need to fret in the wee hours! Don't wait until morning to schedule your day... you may find you have wasted too much time before you "get around to it" and that creates stress as you race against the clock.

Get organized! A cluttered mind produces a cluttered environment. Get rid of clutter and chaos and not only will you feel more in control because you are calmer, you will be much more productive! I currently offer an online course for getting your workplace organized. You can get more information here: www.advantageworkplaceintegration.com/services/online-courses

This was mentioned earlier but it is so important to **give your brain a break several times per day**. Get up, stand up and walk around, stretch. At least 2 times per day, go to that quiet place for 10 minutes, eyes closed and imagine yourself in a peaceful tranquil place and let your mind go there. Don't forget to take 3 deep breaths to begin with to release tension in the neck and shoulders! You want to feel better?

Include humour into your daily routine. Feeding on humour even when you are having a difficult time will release stress, connect you with others, and give your brain a boost!

Feed your brain with positive thoughts. In fact, crowd your brain with them and squeeze out the negative. Think about what is right in your life with gratitude. Remember, neurons that fire together, wire together!

Give yourself **a few seconds of silence** before responding to a stressful situation, to collect your thoughts and avoid saying something that will escalate into a confrontation. Refer to the chapter on conflict.

Don't forget to laugh. It's a great stress reliever.

A good cry can release stress too, in the right setting (not in the workplace, especially in front of your boss please!) Just be sure not to stay there too long. Wipe your tears, take a couple of deep breaths, and carry on!

Protection

Engaging in certain activities can put you at risk for a concussion and brain injury. Whether you are skiing, cycling, riding a motorcycle, skateboarding or participating in other high risk activities, please remember to **wear a properly fitting helmet to protect your precious brain**. I know at times it ruins the mood (can't wear that cute ski hat) or it's just not cool to show up at the skateboarding park wearing one, but just ask someone who lives with a brain injury or who is recovering from concussion and they will urge you to do so! **Injury to the brain can change your life, and it's not pretty, so please be kind to your noggin!**

In addition to wearing a helmet, it is important to **watch out for other people on the roads**. Drivers of vehicles need to accept the fact that motorcycles and bicycles share our roadways and they have the right to do so. Please respect them. Motorcyclists, you should also practice safe operation of your bikes. Be educated in where to position yourself behind vehicles to be seen, always have your head and taillights on, and avoid weaving in and out of traffic. Motorists have difficulty seeing you at the best of times.

This also is true with cyclists. Be sure to follow the rules of the road. I have seen so many cyclists do things like ride the wrong way on a downtown one-way street, try to sneak by a car who has signaled they are turning right, and they try to pass on the right (drivers cannot see you!), and riding two and three abreast on highways. **These activities put you at a great risk.**

Don't be a fool! We all like to have fun. Do not dive into a shallow pool or into any water where you don't know what lurks beneath. It can be shallow, there could be rocks, or much seaweed that can tangle you up and put you at risk of drowning. If you do survive, **loss of oxygen to the brain for a period of time can cause brain damage**. A healthy high school friend of mine showed up at school in a wheelchair. Several weeks earlier he dove into a lake from a low hill, into a bed of rocks on the bottom. He is paralyzed from the neck down. This was avoidable. Again, don't be a fool!

Bottom line – go out and have fun, but come home with your brain intact!!

Change Happens

We have all experienced change in our workplace and in our lives. **How we handle it dictates whether it affects us positively or negatively.** Change is something we all must accept in our lives because the world is changing much faster than ever before and there are no signs of slowing down.

Just think about what your life was like 5 years ago. What type of technology did you use? Who were your friends? A lot of people realize when they look back on an event such as their wedding ceremony, how few of the same people in their lives at that time are still friends now. For example, many people realize most of their wedding party were close at the time but are no longer in their lives. People change, situations change.

Now consider this: of all the things you embrace today, what will be the same in 5 years? Expecting nothing to change is unrealistic. We have a choice... do we fear the changes, or are we excited about great new experiences of the future?

This does not mean everything will change. The things that remain constant generally are how we feel inside, how we treat other people, and our core values. I am a great believer in establishing a set of ethics and principles by which to live, and never waiver. That way we can more easily adapt to our changing world because our standards remain unchanged, creating stability.

Change is here to stay so we might as well accept it... no, let's embrace it! **A few challenges involving change are:**

FEAR - of the unknown. We all have experienced this at some time in our lives. It's a natural human habit.

"Done it the same way for years" mentality

More workload, not enough time

More training, not enough time

Will I lose my job?

Who will be my new manager?

Can I work with new people?

Improper planning can cause chaos for all

Change agents need to be trained as well

Unplanned Changes

Outside influences

Events beyond your control (or the control of your employer) causing actions, processes and opinions to shift

Loss of business

Employee resignation or illness

Generally viewed as negative by management and employees

Planned Changes

Owners/shareholders changing direction
Economic influences (can also be unplanned)
Mergers and acquisitions
Change of location
Generally viewed by management as positive
Generally viewed by employees as negative
(potential disconnect)

The realities of change are many but it's continuous and it's here to stay! Change forces us to rethink our skills, opinions, and processes and adjust. In other words, it is best to be open-minded and flexible.

On the negative side, it can cause immense fear as I said before, creating stress and certainty, zapping our brainpower. We don't like fear of the unknown. It makes us uneasy.

On the positive side, it can create an immense opportunity for personal and professional growth. Embracing change can eliminate old, outdated policies and procedures and attract high-quality talent with fresh ideas.

Embracing change means adjusting our mindset. We must be open to ideas that bring about new ways to improve our workplace and our lives. The "done it this way for years" mentality just does not work anymore. Here are a couple of suggestions that may help you be successful accepting and thriving through change:

Listen to all views.
Understand others' points of view.
Be willing to try something new.

Communicate your concerns and offer solutions (not changing is NOT one of them!) Offer your expertise and assistance on moving into a new direction.

Be the adult in the room. Rise above unproductive negativity.

For the most part you likely cannot stop change. It's much better to jump in and stay positive about the future than to wallow in the past. This will reduce the stress and anxiety around constant change. "If you can't beat 'em, join 'em!"

Successful implementation of change requires careful strategy, communication and inclusiveness. Perhaps the most important aspect is training. Well trained employees are happy employees.

"Train people well enough so they can leave, treat them well enough so they don't want to."
~Richard Branson

If you would like more in depth guidance, register for the online course Management of Change:
www.advantageworkplaceintegration.com/services/online-courses

Workplace Conflict

Worry and fear can zap your brain power. When you have a conflict with someone, do everything you can to resolve it. **There is nothing more taxing to your brain than unresolved issues.** These conflicts can fester and overtake your thoughts, spreading negative energy throughout your body. Unresolved conflict in the workplace will create a tremendous amount of stress. **Here are a few suggestions:**

Pick your battles. We often do not agree with others' opinions, actions or words. It is not necessary to confront everyone. Before you speak or act, consider the consequences. For example, your co-worker is spending too much time on personal phone calls, causing you to get more calls directed at you. This can be handled two ways. One is to tell your manager and let them deal with it, or talk to the person directly. We tend to want to tell the manager. The consequences of that create animosity between you. Perhaps it's better to communicate with them on a non-confrontational basis first. *"I am not sure whether you are aware when you are involved in personal calls I get double* *the calls and I am having difficulty keeping up with it. If you are going to do this, maybe you can cover me for an hour off my phone to catch up."* They will likely get the message and a resolution may be worked out... either they will stop this activity (busted!), or they will take your calls for an hour. If they are not reasonable with your request and continue to abuse their position, then you can go to your manager and tell them you tried to resolve it amicably but they did not co-operate. Always try to resolve issues with the person you have the issue with first. Another example: someone is gossiping about another person and you don't like it. You need to make a judgement call as to whether you should confront it or ignore it. The consequence of confronting it may create a more negative environment for you. Perhaps in this case, ignore it and let it go.

Be considerate to others. Simply displaying respectful actions and words can diffuse an otherwise negative situation. For example, you want to introduce a new process that will benefit your workflow but it may negatively affect someone else's. Bring them into the conversation to seek their input before going ahead with it and they will feel respected and valued, and then work through a compromise that creates consensus.

When you have an issue with someone, go to that person. Do not go to others and talk about them behind their back. This creates a gang mentality that never goes well for anyone. This creates so much negativity and rarely resolves the problem. Go to the person, in person if possible (emails can be misinterpreted and compound the problem) and privately and calmly state your issue. Listen to the other's opinion. Perhaps there has just been a lack of understanding of another's viewpoint or situation and inaccurate assumptions are made. Talk through issues without raising your voice. If they verbally attack you, take a breath before you respond to calm the air and give yourself a moment to respond without reacting. If this is a work situation and it cannot be resolved, then and only then should you bring your manager into the issue to mediate. If it is personal, you can either bring a trusted person in to mediate, or agree to disagree, but leave with an attitude of respect for the other person. Of course, depending on the seriousness of the problem, it may not be possible, but at least make the effort, and then let it go.

Sever toxic relationships. If the other person is toxic to you, then either tell them you cannot continue, or just let them go and do not contact them again. Of course, then it is important for you to emotionally release them from your thoughts. Remember "Take Out the Trash!" **If you would like more assistance on this topic**, you can sign up for my Conflict Resolution online course or schedule an in-office workshop... go here for more info:

www.advantageworkplaceintegration.com/services

Cleaning Up Your Mess!

Perhaps you have taken out the trash after reading Chapter 4. That's great! Are you perfect? We like to think we are, but we know we are not. **If you have messed up, fess up, apologize quickly, make it right, and then forgive yourself.** Your brain will be free to happily focus on something else! That's a mighty tall order, and sometimes it is difficult to do. I guarantee you will feel so much better when you do, and more importantly, you can release that situation and any guilt that goes along with it. Remember, negative thoughts can make us unwell! **Here are a few tips:**

We ALL make mistakes. Some are trivial, and some are doozies! Regardless of how serious it is, finding the courage to go to a person (preferably in person), admitting a wrongdoing and asking for forgiveness is not pleasant at all. We humans tend to avoid unpleasantness by perhaps lying our way out of it and then having to live that lie. When our actions do not align with our thoughts, chaos ensues. This is not recommended!

Doing the right thing, even when it's unpleasant and uncomfortable it's called integrity!

It creates respect and helps to develop your moral code. Do what you say you are going to do, when you say you are going to do it!

When we take ownership of the things we do, positive or negative, we are demonstrating maturity and strength. These traits will carry you through many trials and tribulations going forward. It is much less stressful to do the right thing, than to cover up the wrong. Politicians should take that advice!

As parents, we sometimes don't want to admit our wrongdoings to our kids because they look up to us. Guess what, when we are honest about our mistakes, and ask THEM for forgiveness, they do, because they look up to us! It also teaches them that they will still be loved and forgiven if they come forward to us and admit their mistakes.

Forgive yourself! The late Maya Angelou had this amazing little quote which allows us a pass and can release guilt: *"Do the best you can until you know better, and when you know better, you do better."* – Self-forgiveness and self-love!

Sometimes we cannot "fix" a wrongdoing with another person despite all our efforts. **If you have done everything** you can to remedy the problem without success, it's time to release it and move on. Find peace with yourself and put your energy into more positive activities.

Multi-Tasking!

Are you a proud multi-tasker? Do you believe you are more productive when you take on multiple tasks at once... conserving your precious time? You may be surprised to learn those **who perform one task at a time get more done and with more detail and accuracy!**

We have been almost forced into this way of performing due to our increasingly fast-paced world and it seems taking on more than one task at a time is a necessity. In fact, those who boast they are "great multi-taskers", are **feeling more stressed than those who choose to complete one task at a time**. Multi-tasking is simply a series of distractions!

This can cause sleep problems, mental and physical health issues. This also creates a mindset of "it's not great but good enough", which can cause errors and inefficiency. When performance review time comes, you may be shocked to learn even though you are working "hard", you have not performed as well as you believe.

Multi-tasking has been studied by many and some results suggest **not only can it lower your**

IQ by 15%; it can in fact cause damage to the brain! (This needs more study but the current findings are very troubling.) Refer to https://www.entrepreneur.com/article/244376.

The brain is designed to focus on one task at a time with much brain power being assigned to that task, giving us what we need to complete it. When we switch from one task to another, our brains need to "reboot", therefore interrupting the thought process. When we return to the former task, the brain reboots yet again and cannot just pick up where it left off. It must recall what had transpired before the interruption and that loses precious time. If we are struggling with good memory (due to stress and other factors) we may have to go back and start over from the beginning!

Sometimes multi-tasking habits develop because of attention deficit problems, perhaps caused by prior brain trauma. When the brain experiences a trauma sometimes thinking becomes a bit scrambled, therefore causing us to jump from one activity to another due to inability to focus on a task for very long. If this is the case, it is very important to use **whatever relaxation process that will help calm the brain** and return to more balanced function.

The best way to prevent the tendency to multi-task is to **take the time to get organized and schedule your activities each day (the night before.)** Setting out a plan will help reduce your stress and promote better focus.

Healing Nature

We all know a walk in a forest or along a stream can clear our minds and create a sense of well-being. **It is physically, mentally, emotionally and spiritually healthy to get back to nature.** Working with our hands in a garden or walking barefoot on grass helps to ground us, literally! It sends very calming signals from our feet all the way up to the brain and creates self-regulation. It's all about balance and harmony!

Our brains and bodies are hard-wired to be in sync with nature, such as the sun rise and set (circadian rhythm), and changing seasons, and not 24/7 work schedules! Approximately 70% of the world's population lives in urban areas so it's no wonder **we have an ever-increasing percentage of those with depression, anxiety and sleep disorders**.

Researchers from the Douglas Mental Health University Institute at McGill University in Montreal set out to determine whether changes in neural processes might be responsible for these findings.

They used functional magnetic resonance imaging (fMRI) to monitor the brains of 32 healthy adults asked to complete difficult math problems while being timed and hearing negative verbal responses.

Those who lived in urban environments had increased activity in the amygdala area of the brain, which is involved in emotions such as fear and responses to threats.

Those who lived in cities during the first 15 years of their life also had increased activity in the pregenual anterior cingulate cortex, which helps to regulate the amygdala. In short, **those who grew up in an urban environment had a greater sensitivity to stress**.

To read the full article go to http://articles.mercola.com/sites/articles/archive/2016/08/20/spending-time-in-nature-heals.aspx#_edn14

Per research published in BioPsychoSocial Medicine:

> *"The healing power of nature, vis medicatrix naturae, has traditionally been defined as an internal healing response designed to restore health.*
>
> *Almost a century ago, famed biologist Sir John Arthur Thomson provided an additional interpretation of the word nature within the context of vis medicatrix, defining it instead as the natural, non-built external environment. He maintained that the healing power of nature is also that associated with mindful contact with the animate and inanimate natural portions of the outdoor environment.*

... With global environmental concerns, rapid urban expansion and mental health disorders at crisis levels, diminished nature contact may not be without consequence to the health of the individual and the planet itself."

"Grounding" is becoming more popular, and it is just getting back to connection with nature so the negative electrons in the earth can enter the body with their powerful antioxidant and free-radical busting benefits. Grounding has been shown to relieve pain, reduce inflammation, improve sleep, and enhance your well-being. You can purchase an expensive grounding mat, or preferably just **go outside and walk barefoot in nature**. This is beneficial while walking on surfaces like sand (beach), moist grass, and bare soil or even concrete or brick. There is NO benefit from walking on asphalt, wood, rubber/plastic, or vinyl, or wearing shoes with rubber soles.

Here are some benefits of regular grounding:

Improved sleep.

Reduced stress.

Regulation of autonomic nervous system.

Normalized day/night cortisol rhythm.

Reduced pain.

Wound healing.

Reduced inflammation (one of the major causes of most diseases.)

We should **place a high priority on returning to nature as part of our regular routine**. Find a park, bike path along the river, drive out into rural settings and take a walk, or even garden in your own backyard. When was the last time you walked barefoot in the park? It's fun and can be very freeing!

Brain Buzz

There is so much buzz about the brain lately. It seems everyone is jumping on the brain health bandwagon. **Be very discerning about marketing.** There are products that claim to boost brain power and a few companies have been charged with false advertising. For example, one company added a tiny bit of gingko biloba (not enough to make a difference) to a beverage, and called it a "brain healthy" drink.

There are drugs that also claim to boost brain power. Although they likely have a positive effect, be very careful about side effects, a common occurrence with pharmaceuticals.

The word "brain" or "brain power" is being inserted in advertising that does not have much to do with brain wellness at all. It has become quite trendy. It's important to check out every claim, offering and process of brain wellness products and devices before using. **It is your brain after all and you can find safe ways to keep it healthy.**

There are some very questionable products that claim to elevate your "Theta" waves to encourage creativity and intuition. These can be dangerous mainly because **too much activity of these brain patterns can lead to fear, paranoia, and unrealistic thoughts**.

There is also a buzz about Alpha wave stimulation and although an increased level of function can create happiness and a great sense of self, over-activation can also cause reduced focus and can interrupt sleep. **These two wave patterns optimally should be balanced to each other**, and without having access to technology that can read these patterns, one would not be able to monitor the effects of these devices.

Eat healthy, avoid sugar, starches and processed foods, exercise your body and mind and take time to relax. Follow the suggestions in this book that are right for you, use common sense and you got it covered!

Music Brain

The brain functions in rhythms and therefore responds well to music and many studies support the positive effects musical vibration has on our wellbeing. When music is heard, the brain produces endorphins (feel good) and that is why we all love to listen to our favourite songs.

When we **play an instrument and sing**, we engage our entire brain, not just listening and feeling, but also engaging our **motor skills, cognition, memory, word retrieval, speech centre and more**. An article published in National Geographic in 2014 talks about the benefits of playing an instrument... *"A growing number of studies show that music lessons in childhood can do something perhaps more valuable for the brain than childhood gains: provide benefits for the long run, as we age, in the form of an added defense against memory loss, cognitive decline, and diminished ability to distinguish consonants and spoken words."* Read the entire article:

http://news.nationalgeographic.com/news/2014/0

1/140103-music-lessons-brain-aging-cognitive-neuroscience/

Music therapy is becoming more mainstream to help relieve emotional issues and many psychotherapists are using music as a tool to create positive emotions and a better sense of self. **It is known to also have a positive effect on children who have had a traumatic experience.**

Tempo is a factor in how the brain responds. Fast tempos can create excitement, happiness or anger. Slow tempos can create feelings of contentment and peace, or sadness. Therefore, if you are angry, you may wish to listen to slow-paced music. Or, if you feel a little down, a snappy happy fast-paced song may elevate your mood.

Other factors come into play such as loudness, composition, etc., and drives either a positive or negative response. I find when I listen to music with a tempo of about 1 beat per second (same as a clock,) I feel the most relaxed and content. It will be different for everyone and I invite you to experiment with your own mood and musical choices.

Anyone who plays an instrument or sings regularly knows how very rewarding this is... so exercise those vocal chords or dust off the piano and start playing! (Yes, I sing in my car and don't care what anyone thinks!)

Mind Games

"So keep on playing those mind games." - A quote from a John Lennon song, this chapter does not speak about the kind of mind games we associate with manipulating others, but rather with games and activities that **stimulate the brain**. You may have heard the expression, "Use it or lose it", mostly referring to physical fitness. The same holds true regarding the brain.

There are varying opinions as to whether brain games prevent dementia, so I dare not delve into this topic, but even if they do not, exercising the brain with games, learning a new language or musical instrument **helps the brain make new connections which are beneficial in keeping the brain "sharp", especially as we age**.

Crossword puzzles are good, but there many others that engage the brain in a positive way. **There are brain game apps that are great for exercising the brain and keeping brainwave connections strong.** Many of them will show your progress and are a lot of fun. Give them a try and find the ones you enjoy. **Just make sure you are**

challenging yourself and not just doing the easy ones!

When we engage in these activities and add social interaction with it, such as healthy competition, **we promote a sense of connection and comradery which in turn enhances our mood and self-esteem**.

It is worth noting that engaging in only one game or mind activity limits the overall benefit. We should attempt to **participate in areas that not only enhance our math/sequencing skills, but also our curiosity, reasoning, and artistic aptitude.**

This is not only for those who are aging. Young children all the way up to seniors benefit tremendously from exercising the brain in this way. Since children's brains are very flexible and still developing, introducing a variety of activities and mind stimulation prepares them for life's challenges. They do receive this in school, but should never stop there.

There is much controversy surrounding the benefits of computer-generated games... it depends on the game and the length of time a child is allowed. We certainly do not want to encourage overuse of these games, creating an addictive behaviour, and they should never replace face-to-face social activities and healthy outdoor play.

I do not infer I am an expert on any game or puzzle, and it is always imperative you **do your own research and find the activities that best suit you and your family**. The "brain teaser" type games can be fun, especially when you take up the challenge with others!

This is to simply encourage you to use your brain in a fun way to keep it tuned up!

Relax Your Brain

We have all likely heard about or experienced the benefits of meditation or quiet relaxation. Calming our minds gives our brains a rest and when we can achieve **deep relaxation**, we can cope more effectively with life's challenges.

Chronic stress and lack of quality sleep are at epidemic levels, both of which can create many mental, emotional and physical conditions and illnesses. When we meditate regularly our brains get into the habit of staying calm, and promoting overall wellness.

If your brain is stuck in an overactive or other imbalanced state, however, you may find it difficult to meditate, or even to relax for a few minutes. **Do you lay awake at night with a mind that won't shut off?**

There are processes and devices you can use that create a more relaxed mind resulting in better sleep, and more control over stress. I am happy to offer advice in this regard.

I also offer workplace courses and workshops (www.advantageworkplaceintegration.com/services)

which are productivity/relationship focused and aimed at **working smart and maintaining good wellness**, including the brain.

REMEMBER: TAKE CARE OF YOUR BRAIN, NATURALLY! You will be better equipped to succeed at work and life!

Conclusion

Here is some simple advice: list everything you like and dislike about your job (or personal responsibilities). Wherever possible, do the "dislike" duties first, and do them to the best of your ability. Then when you are doing the tasks you like, do them with flare, enjoying every minute.

For example, I loved meeting with business clients in the field, but really disliked paperwork. I would start my day with paperwork, emails etc. and then had my appointments scheduled for the remainder of the day. This way, those unpleasant tasks were not occupying my mind all day and I could truly enjoy my day... try it!

Happiness is a decision. The only person who can make you happy is you. Put a smile on your face, be positive and excited about the future, and stay true to your values! Have fun!

Resources

Advantage Workplace Integration

Nancy works with those who place high importance on creativity, performance and innovation to ultimately become the employer of choice in their given field.

Loyalty, engagement, enthusiasm, low absenteeism, happiness, productivity, success... does this describe your operation? If not, hire Nancy!

She offers workplace courses and workshops which are productivity/relationship focused and aimed at **working smart and maintaining good wellness**, including the brain:
www.advantageworkplaceintegration.com/services

For information on all services provided by Nancy Attrill, visit AdvantageWorkplaceIntegration.com

Connect with Nancy:

Complimentary Consultation:
www.advantageworkplaceintegration.com/brain-balancing

Facebook: www.facebook.com/LondonABT

LinkedIn: www.linkedin.com/pub/nancy-attrill

About the Author

Nancy Attrill embarked on her professional career several years ago, in various businesses and corporations. Her roles have varied from insurance underwriting to management, marketing and employee training/mentoring, and entrepreneurship. Her focus has always been that of providing world class service through effective, productive and highly motivated teams. She believes strong management skillset is the key to being the employer of choice in each field.

Nancy graduated from Alternative Medicine College of Canada as a Natural Health Consultant and Educator in 2010, specializing in brain health. Her integration of wellness and business expertise offers a unique approach to promote creativity, performance and well-being that her corporate and individual clients greatly embrace.

Nancy provides brain relaxation techniques to individuals and their families to help them overcome the effects of chronic stress and sleep disturbances.

www.ingramcontent.com/pod-product-compliance
Lightning Source LLC
Chambersburg PA
CBHW051819170526
45167CB00005B/2078

* 9 7 8 1 5 4 2 8 5 9 5 8 5 *